William A. Brand

Roll of Honor

The soldiers of Champaign county, who died for the Union

William A. Brand

Roll of Honor
The soldiers of Champaign county, who died for the Union

ISBN/EAN: 9783337308568

Printed in Europe, USA, Canada, Australia, Japan

Cover: Foto ©ninafisch / pixelio.de

More available books at **www.hansebooks.com**

ROLL OF HONOR.

THE

SOLDIERS

OF

CHAMPAIGN COUNTY,

WHO

DIED FOR THE UNION.

COMPILED BY W. A. BRAND.

URBANA, OHIO:
SAXTON & BRAND, PRINTERS.
1876.

A LIST

Of Soldiers who enlisted from Champaign County, Ohio, for service in the Armies of the United States during the war of 1861–5, and who died or were killed in the service:

A

Michael Alderman, Co. C, 66th O. V. I., killed at Port Republic, Va., June 9, 1862. Buried in Staunton National Cemetery as Unknown.

Milton Alien, Co. K, 66th O. V. I., died at David's Island, N. Y., Nov. 26, 1862. Buried at Cypress Hill Cemetery.

David Apple, Co. H, 45th O. V. I., killed at Knoxville, Tenn., Nov. 15, 1863. Buried at Knoxville National Cemetery.

Cephas Atkinson, Co. E, 95th O. V. I., died at Memphis, Tenn., Mch. 22, 1865. Buried as Unknown, at Vicksburg National Cemetery.

Ezra Allen, corporal, Co. K, 113th O. V. I., killed at Kenesaw Mountain, June 27, 1864. Buried in National Cemetery at Marietta, Ga., among the unknown.

Wm. R. Arrowsmith, Co. H, 45th O. V. I., captured by the enemy Nov. 15, 1863, and died in Andersonville prison, Ga., Sept. 28, 1864. Buried in Andersonville National Cemetery.

Reuben M. Alden, Co. C, 134th O. N. G., wounded June 17, 1864, and died at Hampton, Va., June 23. Buried in Hampton National Cemetery.

Norval W. Anderson, Co. A, 2d O. V. I.,
killed at Stone River, Tenn., Dec. 30,
1862. Buried in National Cemetery on
the battle-field: initials on tombstone,
"N—W—A—"

Henry Ames, Sergeant, Co. I, 66th O. V. V. I.,
wounded at Port Republic, Va., June 9,
1862; died at Chattanooga, Tenn., June
21, 1864. Buried in Chattanooga National Cemetery.

James Allman, Co. A, 2d O. V. I., exchanged
prisoner of war, lost in the burning of
the steamer Sultana, April 27, 1865.

John Abbott, Co. C, 66th O. V. I., contracted pulmonary disease in the service and
lingered till 1873—dying at home.

B

John Blue, Co. E, 45th O. V. I ,died at Lexington, Ky., Feb. 4, 1863. Buried at home.

David Blue, Co. H, 26th O. V. I., died at
Nashville, Tenn., July 1, 1863. Buried
in Nashville National Cemetery.

Miles C. Baker, Co. H, 26th O. V. I., died in
West Virginia, Nov. — 1861. Buried at
home.

Wm. Brasket, Co. E, 113th O. V. I., died at
Chattanooga, Tenn., Mch. 1, 1864. Buried
in Chattanooga National Cemetery.

Henry Brittin, Co. K, 113th O. V. I., died in
Chattanooga, Tenn., July 6, 1864. Buried
in Chattanooga National Cemetery.

Charles Bartholomew, Co. H, 26th O. V. I.,
killed at Stone River, Tenn., Dec. 31,
1862. Buried at National Cemetery on
battle ground.

George Brewster, Co. H, 26th O. V. I., died in Virginia, Sept. 16, 1861. Place of death and place of burial unknown.

John Brown, Co. I, 66th O. V. I., died at Martinsburg, Va., May 15, 1862. Buried in Winchester Nationa' Cemetery as Unknown.

James Boulton, Co. I, 66th O. V. I , died at Alexandria, Va., Aug. 9, 1862. Buried at home.

Wm. L. Butler, Co. G, 66th O. V. I., killed at Chancellorsville, Va., May 3, 1863. Buried as Unknown in Fredericksburg National Cemetery.

Lewis Bedell, Co. B, 66th O. V. I., died at Newark, O., Jan. 17, 1863.

Jeremiah Blocher, Co. C, 66th O. V. I., died at Annapolis, Md., Oct. 1, 1862. Buried in Annapolis National Cemetery.

Lucas Burnham, Co. G, 95th O. V. I., died at Walnut Hills, Miss., July 23, 1863. Buried in National Cemetery at Vicksburg as Unknown.

Samuel Blue, Co. G, 3d Ohio Cavalry, died at home, Dec. 3, 1862.

Christopher Baxter, Co. I, 66th O. V. I., died at home, Jan. 5, 1864, of disease contracted in service.

Peter M. Black, Co. C, 12th Ohio Cav., wounded at Cynthiana, Ky., and died of wounds July 25, 1864, at Mt. Sterling. Burial place unknown.

W. D. Bartlett, Co. E, 11th Kansas Inf., died at Manhattan, Kan., Aug. 24, 1865. Burial place unknown.

Wm. E. Best, Co. A, 66th O. V. I., wounded in leg at Port Republic, Va., June 9, 1862; amputation at Cliffborne Hospital resulted in death July 24, 1862. Buried in Military Asylum National Cemetery.

James Burns, Co. K, 66th O. V. I., died in Columbus, O., Feb. 29, 1864. Buried in Green Lawn Cemetery.

John R. Baldwin, Sergeant, Co. G, 66th O. V. I., died in Washington, D. C., June 18, 1862. Buried in Oak Dale Cemetery.

Stephen Baxter, Sergeant, Co. I. 66th O. V. I., killed at Port Republic, Va., June 9, 1862. Buried among the unknown in Staunton National Cemetery.

Francis M. Brittin, Co. I, 66th O. V. V. I., died at Nashville, Tenn., Nov. 20, 1864, of wounds received at Peach Tree Creek, Ga., July 20, 1864. Buried in Nashville National Cemetery.

Amos Brown, Co. C, 66th O. V. I., was captured by the enemy at Port Republic, Va., June 9, 1862; from the effects of imprisonment he died at Annapolis, Md., Oct. 1, 1862. Buried in Annapolis National Cemetery.

Luke W. Bryant, Co. A, 66th O. V. I., a paroled prisoner of war, died at Camp Parole, Annapolis, Md., Feb. 25, 1863. Buried at home.

Enos Brown, Co. C, 66th O. V. I., was wounded at Cedar Mountain, Va., Aug. 9, 1862. He died at Alexandria, Va., Mch. 28, 1864. Buried in National Cemetery at Alexandria.

Wm. Beltz, Co. H, 66th O. V. I., died at Alexandria, Va., June 30, 1862. Buried in the Alexandria National Cemetery.

Wm. Wallace Baird, Co. G, 66th O. V. I., killed at Ringold, Ga., Nov. 27, 1863. Buried in Chattanooga National Cemetery.

Samuel C. Brinnin, Co. I, 66th O. V.V. I., killed at Peach Tree Creek, Ga., July 20, 1864. Buried at Marietta National Cemetery.

Wm. J. Blair, Co. A, 66th O. V. I., wounded at Cedar Mountain, Va., Aug. 9, 1862; killed at Chancellorsville, Va., May 3, 1863. Buried among the unknown in Fredericksburg National Cemetery.

Edward B. Bartlett, Co. G, 66th O. V. I., died at Harpers Ferry, Va., Dec. 26, 1862. Buried as Unknown in Winchester National Cemetery.

Andrew Black, Co. A, 66th O. V. I., killed at Port Republic, Va., June 9, 1862. Buried among the unknown in Staunton National Cemetery.

John K. Briney, Co. A, 66th O. V. I., killed at Port Republic, Va., June 9, 1862. Buried among the unknown in Staunton National Cemetery.

Stephen V. Barr, Co. K, 113th O. V. I., killed at Kenesaw Mountain, Ga., June 27, 1864. Buried in Marietta National Cemetery.

Peter Baker, Co. E, 113th O. V. I., died at Nashville, Tenn., Aug. 15, 1864, of wounds received at Kenesaw Mountain, Ga., June 27, 1864. Buried in Nashville National Cemetery.

Geo. A. Baker, Co. E, 113th O, V. I., died at Nashville, Tenn., Mch. 20, 1863. Buried in Nashville National Cemetery.

John H. Bricker, Co. K, 113th O. V. I., killed near Chattahoochie river, Ga., July 4, 1864. Originally buried at Vining's Station; removed to National Cemetery at Marietta.

John Bowersock, Captain, 113th O. V. I., killed at Kenesaw Mountain, Ga., June 27, 1864. Buried at home.

Wm. Bower, Co. E. 95th O. V. I., prisoner of war from Guntown, Miss., confined in Andersonville, Ga., and died of starvation. Buried in Andersonville National Cemetery.

E. C. Brecount, 94th O..V. I., was wounded at Perryville, Ky., and died Oct. 14, 1862. Buried at home.

John B. Benedict, Co. F, 31st O. V. I., died at Camp Nelson, Ky., March 1, 1862. Buried originally at Lebanon, Ky., and subsequently removed to his home.

Charles Breedlove, Co. F, 54th O. V. I., died at Savannah, Tenn., April 15, 1862. Buried in National Cemetery at Shiloh.

Daniel Banen, Co. D, 2d O. V. I., died at Louisville, Ky., Feb. 15, 1862. Buried in Cave Hill Cemetery.

Wm. P. Bain, Co. D, 66th O. V. I., killed at Port Republic, Va., June 9, 1862. Buried in Staunton National Cemetery as Unknown.

Abraham Branstitter, Co. A, 2d O. V. I., died at Huntsville, Ala., June 2, 1862. Burial place unknown.

A. S. Berryhill, Captain, 2d O. V. I., killed at Perryville, Ky., Oct. 8, 1862. Buried in National Cemetery on the battle ground, as "Capt—Berrywood—Ohio."

Jerry Brown, Co. A, 27th U. S. Colored Troops, killed in storming a Fort in front of Petersburg, Va., July 30, 1864. No burial.

John Barrett, Co. A, 27th U. S. Colored Troops, killed in storming a Fort in front of Petersburg, Va., July 30, 1864. No burial.

Richard W. Baldwin, Co. F, 134th O. N. G., died at Hampton, Va., Aug. 22, 1864. Buried in Hampton National Cemetery, and subsequently removed to Oak Dale Cemetery.

Samuel H. Blake, Co. B, 32d O. V. I., died of wounds received in front of Atlanta, Ga., July 22, 1864. Buried in Marietta National Cemetery as Unknown.

J. M. Butcher, Captain, 30th Ind. Inf., died at home, Dec. 1, 1865, of wounds, and disease contracted in the service.

Wilson Brittin, Co. I, 66th O. V. I., died at Harpers Ferry, Va., Dec. —, 1862. Buried in National Cemetery at Winchester, Va., as Unknown.

Lilburn C. Brown, —— 94th O. V. I., supposed to have died near Milliken's Bend, La. He was left sick at a farm house, and has never been heard from.

John Barbee, —— 20th O. V. I., killed July 22, 1864, near Atlanta, Ga. Buried in Marietta National Cemetery—supposed grave marked "J.—B.—"

Jacob Brothers, Co. B, 32d O. V. I., died June 27, 1865, and is buried in the National Cemetery at Parkersburg, W. Va.

S. W. Brown, Co. C, 13th O. V. I., died at Nashville, Tenn., Oct. 5, 1862. Buried in National Cemetery at that place.

Wm. H. Beck, Co. D, 13th O. V. I., died at New Albany, Ind., Oct. 13, 1862. Buried in New Albany National Cemetery.

Peter K. Blagg, Co. I, 13th O, V. I., died in Cincinnati, O , Nov. 10, 1862. Buried in Spring Grove Cemetery.

J. P. Born, Co. G, 134th O. N. G., died at Point of Rocks, Va., July 29, 1864. Buried in City Point National Cemetery.

Elias Busser, Co. A, 134th O. N. G., killed on skirmish line, in front of Petersburg, Va., June 17, 1864. Buried at home.

John R. Brown, Lieutenant, 13th Ohio Battery, died in Urbana, O., May 29, 1862. Buried in Oak Dale Cemetery.

Jacob Black, Co. G, 95th O. V. I., wounded at Vicksburg, and is supposed to have died in some hospital unknown to his friends and comrades.

Elias Branstitter, Co. B, 66th O. V. I., died at home, of disease contracted in the service. Date unknown.

C

Samuel Connor, Co. G, 3d Ohio Cavalry, died at Savannah, Tenn., —— —— Buried in National Cemetery at Shiloh, Miss.

Jas. A. Caruthers, Co. G, 95th O. V. I., died at home, March 10, 1865.

Zachariah Cox, Co. H, 45th O. V. I., died at Knoxville, Tenn., Nov. 24, 1863. Buried in Knoxville National Cemetery as Unknown.

Christopher C. Cranston, Co. A, 2d O. V. I., killed at Stone River, Tenn., Dec. 31, 1862. Buried in National Cemetery on battle ground; grave marked "G. G. Granston."

Julius J. Cushman, Co. A, 2d O. V. I., wounded at Hoover's Gap, Tenn., June 25, 1862; died of wounds same day. Buried in National Cemetery at Stone River.

Jasper Carter, Co. A, 2d O. V. I., killed at Resacca, Ga., May 14, 1864. Buried in National Cemetery at Chattanooga.

Darius Comer, Co. I, 42d O. V. I., died at New Orleans, La., Feb. 1, 1864. Buried at home.

David J. Comer, Co, I. 42d O. V. I., died at home, Oct. 6, 1863.

J. H. Corwin, Co. I, 42d O. V. I., killed in seige of Vicksburg, Miss. Burial place unknown.

Jacob Cox, Co. C, 66th O. V. I., killed at Port Republic, Va., June 9, 1862. Buried as Unknown in Staunton National Cemetery.

J. M. Cookes, Co. I, 66th O. V. I., killed at Port Republic, Va., June 9, 1862. Buried as Unknown in Staunton National Cemetery.

Ross Colwell, Co. H, 66th O. V. I., died at Harpers Ferry, Va., Nov. 16, 1862. Buried in Oak Dale Cemetery.

George Conrad, Co. E, 113th O. V. I., died at Nashville, Tenn., May 10, 1863. Buried in Nashville National Cemetery.

Wm. H. H. Cook, Co. G, 66th O. V. I., wounded at Cedar Mountain, Va., Aug. 9, 1862, and died of wounds at Alexandria, Va., August 28, 1862. Buried in Alexandria National Cemetery.

Geo. G. Connor, Co. G, 95th O. V. I., died at Black River Hospital, Miss., July 1, 1863. Buried in Vicksburg National Cemetery as Unknown.

Jno. W. Cawood, Sergt., Co. E, 95th O. V. I., killed at Guntown, Miss., June 10, 1864. Buried as Unknown in Vicksburg National Cemetery.

Jos. Coleman, Co. G, 95th O. V. I., captured by the enemy at Guntown, Miss., June 10, 1864, and murdered same day for his watch. Buried in Andersonville National Cemetery.

L. J. Coverstone, Co. E, 95th O. V. I., died on board hospital steamer Wood, July 3, 1863. Buried in Memphis National Cemetery.

James R. Coulter, Lt., 95th O. V. I., wounded at Vicksburg; died at Memphis, Tenn., Nov. 9, 1864. Buried in Oak Dale Cemetery.

Wm. G. Carpenter, Co. E, 113th O. V. I., killed at Chickamauga, Ga., Sept. 20, 1863. Buried as Unknown in Chattanooga National Cemetery.

Francis M. Cloud, Co. H, 113th O. V. I., killed at Big Shanty, Ga., June 30, 1864. Buried in Marietta National Cemetery.

Thos. Coleman, Co. H, 26th O. V. I., killed at Chickamauga, Ga., Sept. 19, 1863. Buried in Chattanooga National Cemetery as Unknown.

Wm. Crawford, Co. G, 95th O. V. I., died Sept. 5, 1862, of wounds received at Richmond, Ky. Buried in Richmond Cemetery as Unknown.

Edward Camp, Co. B, 66th O. V. I., died in Clarke county, O., Jan. 8, 1864.

Patrick Connell, Co. H, 26th O. V. I., killed at Chickamauga, Ga., Sept. 19, 1863. Buried in Chattanooga National Cemetery as Unknown.

Samuel Carl, Co. F, 54th O. V. I., killed at Shiloh, April 6, 1862. Buried in Pittsburg Landing National Cemetery as Unknown.

Wm. Coppin, Co. K, 113th O. V. I., killed at Kenesaw Mountain, Ga., June 27, 1864. Buried in Marietta National Cemetery as Unknown.

Geo. W. Cushman, Co. H, 66th O. V. I., died at Nashville, Tenn., May 12, 1864. Buried in Nashville National Cemetery.

John Chatfield, Co. H, 66th O. V. I., died at Martinsburg, Va., March 20, 1862. Buried in National Cemetery at Winchester.

Wm. V. Colwell, Co. H, 66th O. V. I., died at home, April 8, 1862. Buried in Oak Dale Cemetery.

Wm. B. Cutler, Co. B, 66th O. V. I., died at Winchester, Va., ———— 1862. Buried at Terrehaute.

Samuel Curl, Co. --, 54th O. V. I., killed at Pittsburg Landing, April 6, 1862. Buried in National Cemetery on the battle field.

Wm. W. Campbell, Co. H, 66th O. V. I.; died at Philadelphia, Pa., Dec. 21, 1862. Buried in Philadelphia Cemetery.

G. L. Chidester, Co. A., 66th O. V. I., killed at Port Republic, Va., June 9, 1862. Buried among the unknown in Staunton National Cemetery.

Wm. Campbell, Co. A, 66th O. V. I., killed at Port Republic, Va., June 9, 1862. Buried as Unknown in Staunton National Cemetery.

Harrison Crouch, Co. G, 134th O. N. G., died at home, Sept. 1, 1864.

Lafayette Clem, Co. H, 134th O. N. G., died at home, Aug. 31, 1864.

Jacob F. Connor, corporal, Co. C, 12th Ohio Cavalry, killed at Mt. Sterling, Ky., June 12, 1864. Buried in Camp Nelson National Cemetery.

Frank T. Coles, Co. C, 4th Ohio Cavalry, killed near Atlanta, Ga., Aug. 20, 1864. Buried in National Cemetery at Marietta as Unknown.

Armisted Claspy, 12th Mich. Inf., died at Nashville, Tenn., Sept. —, 1863. Buried in Nashville National Cemetery.

Edwin S. Crawford, Co. F, 6th O. V. I., died at Nashville, Tenn., Sept. 3, 1862. Buried in Nashville National Cemetery, and afterwards removed to Cemetery at Woodstock, O.

Daniel G. Coleman, Lieut. in "Squirrel Hunters," was killed on the C. H. & D. R. R., Sept. 4, 1862. Buried at home.

M. W. Cilley, Co. I, 66th O. V. I., wounded at Cedar Mountain, Va., Aug. 9, 1862, and died of wounds at Alexandria, Va., Sept. 8, 1862. Buried in Alexandria National Cemetery.

Peter Cox, Co. G, 66th O. V. V. I., thrice wounded at New Hope Church, Ga., May 27, 1864, and died at Nashville, Tenn., of wounds, Sept. 20, 1864. Buried in Nashville National Cemetery.

—— Colwell, Co. G, 3d Ohio Cavalry, killed on Cumberland Mountain, Ga., Sept. 14, 1862. Buried as Unknown in Chattanooga National Cemetery.

—— Cramer, Co. G, 3d Ohio Cavalry, died at Decatur, Ala., July 1, 1862.

Thomas Crouch, Co. L, 2d Ohio Heavy Artillery, died at Knoxville Tenn., —— —— Buried as Unknown in Knoxville National Cemetery.

John B. Cartmell, Co. B, 32d O. V. I., died at home, Oct. 20, 1862, of disease contracted in service.

Jac. Cook, Co. E, 185th O. V. I., died at Louisville, Ky., Mch. 15, 1865. Buried in Cave Hill National Cemetery.

Amos Clark, Co. C, 13th O. V. I., died in 1862, at Urbana, O. Burial place unknown.

Hugh Christy, Co. C, 66th O. V. I., died in a Confederate prison, place and date unknown.

James Cawood, Co. G., 66th O. V. I., died at home, Nov. 30, 1862.

Wm. Cameron, Co. H, 26th O. V. I., died Oct. 22, 1863,—place unknown.

D

Harry Davis, Lieut., 66th O. V. I., wounded at Cedar Mountain, Va., Aug. 9, 1862; killed at Ringold, Ga., Nov. 27, 1863, in charge upon the face of Taylor's Ridge. Buried at home.

Booker Darnell, Co. K, 113th O. V. I., missing after charge on Kenesaw Mountain, Ga., June 27, 1864; supposed to have been killed. Burial place unknown.

John H. Duncan, Co. I, 113th O. V. I., died at Nashville, Tenn., Oct. 15, 1864. Buried in National Cemetery at that place.

Oliver P. Devore, Co. H, 66th O. V. I., died at Alexandria, Va., Aug. — 1862. Buried in National Cemetery at Alexandria.

Wm T. Davis, Co. H, 66th O. V. I., died at Winchester, Va., April 12, 1862. Buried at home.

Francis Deshnier, Co. B, 66th O. V. I., was wounded at Ringold, Ga., Nov. 27, 1863, and died at Chattanooga, Tenn., Dec. 1, 1863. Buried in Chattanooga National Cemetery.

Zarah C. Davis, Co. E, 45th O. V. I., killed at Nashville, Tenn., Dec. 5, 1864. Buried in Nashville National Cemetery.

Stephen Dysart, Co. E, 1st Bat. 15th U. S. Inf., died at Nashville, Tenn., March 25, 1862. Buried in Nashville National Cemetery.

Smith Davis, Co. G, 3d Ohio Cavalry, died at Nashville, Tenn., —— 1862. Buried in Nashville National Cemetery as "S. Davis."

E. C. Davies, Sergt., Co. A, 134th O. N. G., died at Point of Rocks, Va., July 28, 1864. Buried at Oak Dale Cemetery.

John 'Dunham, Co. A, 134th O. N. G., died at Point of Rocks, Va., July 15, 1864. Buried at City Point National Cemetery.

James Dodson, 99th O. V. I, died in Andersonville prison, Ga., Sept. 15, 1864. Buried in Andersonville National Cemetery.

Geo. W. Davis, killed in Tennessee, supposed to have been in 44th Ohio Inf.

Oscar H. Dow, Co. G, 66th O. V. I., wounded at Cedar Mountain, Va., Aug. 9, 1862, and died at Alexandria, Va., Sept. 8, 1862, of his wounds. Buried in Alexandria National Cemetery.

Daniel Derrickson, Co. B, 66th O. V. I., shot by a rebel on Banks' retreat in May, 1862, between Strasburg and Winchester, Va. Buried as Unknown in Winchester National Cemetery.

Samuel F. Diltz, Co. A, 66th O. V. I., died at Cumberland, Md., Feb. 20, 1862. Buried at home.

E

David H. Espy, Co. G, 66th O. V. I., wounded at Cedar Mountain, Va., Aug. 9, 1862; amputation of leg resulted in death at Washington, D. C., Oct. —, 1862. Buried in National Cemetery at Washington.

Monroe Elliott, Co. K, 2d O. V. I., three months service; Lieut. Co. H, 66th O. V. I., severely wounded at Cedar Mountain, Va., Aug. 9, 1862, and discharged for disability; Sergt. Co. K, 113th O. V. I., died at Savannah, Ga., Jan. —, 1864. Buried in National Cemetery at Beaufort, S. C.

Levi Elliott, Co. K, 113th O. V. I., died at Nashville, Tenn., Aug. 12, 1864. Buried in National Cemetery at Nashville.

Benjamin Evans, Co. C, 66th O. V. I., died at Washington, D. C., Jan. —, 1864. Buried in Military Asylum National Cemetery.

Thomas G. Eccles, Co. H, 66th O. V. I., prisoner of war from Front Royal, Va., April 6, 1862, to Sept. 1862; died in Nashville, Tenn., Aug. 27, 1864. Buried in Nashville National Cemetery.

Lewis Everett, Co. C, 66th O. V. I., died at Atlanta, Ga., Nov. 3, 1864. Buried in Marietta National Cemetery.

Daniel Eaton, Co. H, 66th O. V. I., killed at Ringold, Ga., in charge upon Taylor's Ridge, Nov. 27, 1863.

Daniel Eicher, Co. B, 20th O. V. I., died at home, Nov. 2, 1865, of effects of imprisonment at Florence, S. C., and Andersonville, Ga.

Wat. Evans, Co. G, 3d Ohio Cavalry, was killed in 1862, on the cars in Kentucky. Place of death and burial unknown.

John Edwards, Co. H, 45th O. V. I., prisoner of war, died in Richmond, Va., Mch. 21, 1864. Buried in Richmond National Cemetery.

Samuel Everett, Corporal, Co. A, 2d O. V. I., killed in battle of Lookout Mountain, Ga., Nov. 24, 1863. Buried in Chattanooga National Cemetery.

Moses Everett, Co. H, 45th O. V. I., was captured by the enemy at Philadelphia, Tenn., Oct. 20, 1863, exchanged in 1864, and died at home, March 30, 1865.

F

Wm. C. Flago, Sergt., Co. B, 66th O. V. I., (Commissioned Lieutenant) was killed at Chancellorsville, Va, May 3, 1863. Buried among the Unknown in Fredericksburg National Cemetery.

Isaiah Fuson, Co. E, 95th O. V. I., died at Young's Point, La., May 24, 1863. Buried as Unknown in Memphis National Cemetery.

Patrick Fields, Co. K, 113th O. V. I., was wounded at Kenesaw Mountain, Ga., June 27, 1864, and died at Nashville, Tenn., Aug. 19, 1864. Buried in Nashville National Cemetery.

Geo. Finch, Co. H, 45th O. V. I., died at Covington, Ky., Oct. 19, 1862. Buried in Covington National Cemetery.

S. J. Fritz, Co. G, 3d Ohio Cavalry, died at Louisville, Ky., Sept. 28, 1862. Buried in Cave Hill National Cemetery.

Francis M. Fields, Co. H, 45th O. V. I., accidentally shot while on picket, near Somerset, Ky., May 17, 1863. Burial place unknown.

Dr. J. Faulkner, Co. G, 3d Ohio Cavalry, died at home, Oct. —, 1861.

Michael Fritz, Co. A, 2d O. V. I., died at Nashville, Tenn., Sept. 9, 1862; was in Co. K, 2d O. V. I., three months service. Buried in Nashville National Cemetery.

Felix Fisher, Co. I, 96th O. V. I., died at Jefferson Barracks, Mo., April 17, 1863. Buried in National Cemetery at that place.

Crea Finch, Co. K, 66th O. V. I., died at Annapolis, Md., Jan. 6, 1863. Buried in National Cemetery at Camp Parole.

Jas. R. Forsythe, Co. A, 66th O. V. V. I., died at Savannah, Ga., Jan. 3, 1865. Buried in Beaufort National Cemetery.

Nicholas Fiegle, Co. G, 3d Ohio Cavalry, killed Aug. 3, 1862, while on picket near Gunther's Landing, Ala. Burial place unknown.

G

Wm. Gowdy, Co. H, 26th O. V. I., wounded at Chickamauga, Ga., Sept. 19, 1863, arm amputated at shoulder; died Oct. 2, 1863. Burial place unknown.

Lewis Green, Sergt., Co. G, 113th O. V. I., killed at Kenesaw Mountain, Ga., June 27, 1864. Buried in Marietta National Cemetery.

Levi Gladden, Co. A, 66th O. V. I., killed at Port Republic, Va., June 9, 1862. Buried as Unknown in Staunton National Cemetery.

Newton Gray, Co. A, 66th O. V. I., died at Cypress Hill, Long Island, Nov. 3, 1862. Buried in Cypress Hill National Cemetery.

John B. Grove, Co. B, 66th O. V. I., died at Urbana, O., —— —— Buried in Oak Dale Cemetery.

Francis Gardner, Co. B, 32d O. V. I., died at Beverly, Va., Dec. 31, 1861. Burial place unknown.

Ezra Grafton, Co. C, 66th O. V. I., died at St. Paris, O., March —, 1862. Buried at home.

Adolphus Green, Co. G, 95th O. V. I., wounded at Richmond, Ky., and died Sept. 6, 1862. Burial place unknown.

Wm. Gray, Corp., Co. I, 42d O. V. I., mortally wounded at Grand Gulf, Miss., May. 10, 1863. Buried in Vicksburg National Cemetery.

Elias Grove, Co. G, 3d Ohio Cavalry, died at Knoxville, Tenn., Sept. 28, 1864. Buried in National Cemetery at that place.

Wm. R. Gilbert, Co. E, 185th O. V. I., died at Louisville, Ky., Mch. 26, 1865. Buried in Cave Hill National Cemetery.

Jasper N. Ganson, Co. A, 66th O. V. I., died at home, April 23, 1865, of disease contracted in the service.

Isaac Graham, Co. C, 12th Ohio Cavalry, died at Camp Nelson, Ky., Dec. 31, 1864. Buried at home.

Asa Grant, Co. C, 134th O. N. G., died at City Point, Va., July 22, 1864. Buried in City Point National Cemetery.

Isaiah Gales, Co. A, 27th U. S. Colored Troops, died in Philadelphia, Pa., Sept. 26, 1864. Buried in Philadelphia Cemetery.

Henry S. Gingery, Co. B, 113th O. V. I., wounded near Atlanta, Ga., Aug. 9, 1864, and died at Chattanooga, Tenn., Sept. 2, 1864. Buried in Chattanooga National Cemetery.

Jas. Harper Gowdy, Corporal, Co. A. 2d O. V. I., wounded at Resacca, Ga., May 14, 1864; died of wounds at Nashville, Tenn., June 7, 1864. Buried in Nashville National Cemetery.

John W. Greene, Co. A. 2d O. V. I., died at Antioch Church, Nov. 6, 1862, of wounds received at Perryville, Ky., Oct. 8, 1862. Buried in National Cemetery at Perryville.

S. W. Grove, Co. H, 45th O. V. I., prisoner of war from Knoxville, Tenn., died in Richmond, Va., Feb. 1, 1864. Buried in Richmond National Cemetery.

H

Thomas B. Hartshorne, Co. D, 114th O. V. I., died in Madison Parish, La., April 25, 1863. Buried in Vicksburg National Cemetery.

Erastus Hall, Co. I, 66th O. V. I., died at home of disease contracted in the service. Date unknown.

Marcus Hazel, of Harrison township, was in the Mississippi Marine Service, and was killed on a gunboat. Date unknown.

Charles Holmes, Co. C, 33d U. S. Colored Troops, killed in South Carolina, Sept. 23, 1863. Buried in National Cemetery at Beaufort, S. C.

Geo. Hoffman, of Goshen township, died in 1862. Regiment unknown.

Jacob Hudson, Co. H, 66th O. V. I., killed at
Cedar Mountain, Va., Aug. 9, 1862. Bu-
ried among the Unknown in Culpeper
National Cemetery.

Stephen R. Hutchinson, Co. G, 95th O. V. I.,
died in Cincinnati, O., Oct. 24, 1862, of
wounds received at Richmond, Ky. Buried in Spring Grove Cemetery.

Oliver Henry, Co. E, 95th O. V. I., captured
by the enemy at Guntown, Miss., June
10, 1864; exchanged at the mouth of
the Savannah river and died on board
·transport "Geo. Leary," Nov. 26, 1864.

Benjamin Herr, Co. G, 95th O. V. I., died at
Oak Ridge, Miss., Sept. 11, 1863. Buried
in Vicksburg National Cemetery as Unknown.

Geo. W. Henry, Co. E, 95th O. V. I., captured by the enemy and died in Andersonville prison, May 4, 1864. Buried in
Andersonville National Cemetery.

Will C. Harris, Co. C, 94th O. V. I., wounded at Resacca, Ga., May 14, 1864; died
at Chattanooga, Tenn., July 21, 1864.
Buried in Chattanooga National Cemetery.

B. F. Howell, Co. G, 44th O. V. I., shot in
Louisville, Ky., Dec. 12, 1864. Buried
in Cave Hill National Cemetery.

John S. Hendrix, 110th O. V. I., wounded
near Frederick City, Md., July 9, 1864,
died Aug. 11, 1864. Buried at home.

Scott Hill, Co. G, 66th O. V. I., died at Cumberland, Md., Feb. 17, 1862. Buried as
Unknown in Antietam National Cemetery.

Patrick Hannagan, Co. C, 66th O. V. I., wounded at Port Republic, Va., June 9, 1862, and died of fever, arising from wounds, at Alexandria, Va., July 24, 1862. Buried in Alexandria National Cemetery.

Wm. O. Hunter, Co. H, 66th O. V. I., died at Martinsburg, Va., April 13th, 1862. Buried in National Cemetery at Winchester.

Dwight Horr, Co. I, 66th O. V. I., wounded at Port Republic, Va., June 9, 1862, and died of wounds in Washington, D. C., July 7, 1862. Buried at home.

Reuben Hoffman, Co. C, 66th O. V. I., died at Camp McArthur, near Urbana, Dec. 2, 1861. Buried in Oak Dale Cemetery.

Flemon Hall, Co. C, 66th O. V. I., captured by the enemy at Winchester, Va., in May, 1862, and died in prison at Lynchburg, Va., in July. Buried in Poplar Grove National Cemetery, near Petersburg, Va.

Wm. Hess, Co. I, 66th O. V. I., died in Washington, D. C., Oct. 11, 1862. Buried in Military Asylum National Cemetery.

Thomas Hudson, Co. G, 95th O. V. I., died at Vicksburg, Miss., Oct. 22, 1863. Buried in Vicksburg National Cemetery.

John Q. Holland, Sergt., Co. C, 13th O, V. I., killed at Stone River, Tenn., Dec. 31, 1862. Buried in National Cemetery on battle ground as Unknown.

John H. Hunter, Co. G, 95th O. V. I., died at Memphis, Tenn., Mch. 27, 1865. Buried in Memphis National Cemetery.

Henry Harrison Hess, Co. K, 2d O. V. I., (3 months) captured by the enemy at Bull Run, July 21, 1861 ; was a prisoner in Richmond, Va., Salisbury, N. C., New Orleans, La. He was paroled at Richmond, Va., in 1862, and from the effects of his long imprisonment, he died at home, June 19, 1862.

Wm. G. Harper, Co. F, 54th O. V. I., wounded near Paducah, Ky., April 6, 1862, captured by the enemy and confined at Macon, Ga. After his parole, and while making his way to the Federal lines, he died at Petersburg, Va., Oct. 1, 1862. Buried as Unknown in Poplar Grove National Cemetery, near Petersburg, Va.

Pat. Howard, Co. A, 66th O. V. I., mortally wounded at Port Republic, Va., June 9, 1862. Died June 12, at Weyers Cave. Supposed to be buried with the unknown in Staunton National Cemetery.

D. Merrill Humes, Co. A, 66th O. V. I., captured by the enemy at Port Republic, Va., June 9, 1862, confined in prison at Belle Isle, near Richmond, Va., until Sept. 5, 1862. From the effects of his imprisonment he died at Fort Delaware, Oct. 27, 1862. Buried in Oak Dale Cemetery.

John S. Heflebower, 17th Ohio Battery, drowned at Vicksburg, Miss., Aug. ·23, 1863.

Alex. Henry, Co. B, 113th O. V. I., killed in Maryland, June 12, 1865, by falling from cars.

Joseph W. Hitt, Lieutenant, 66th, O. V. I., captured by the enemy at Port Republic, Va., June 9, 1862, exchanged Sept. 5, 1862; killed in action at New Hope Church, Ga., May 25, 1864, in performance of his duty as Aide-de-Camp to Brigade Commander. Buried in Oak Dale Cemetery.

Reuben Humbert, Co. C, 66th O. V. I., killed at New Hope Church, Ga., May 28, 1864. Buried as Unknown in Marietta National Cemetery.

Rolven Huddleston, Co. E, 113th O. V. I., killed at Chickamauga, Ga., Sept. 20, 1863. Buried in Chattanooga National Cemetery as Unknown.

Jacob Hess, Co. E, 113th O. V. I., killed at Kenesaw Mountain, Ga., June 27, 1864. Buried in Marietta National Cemetery as Unknown.

Hiram Hancock, Co. K, 113th O. V. I., killed at Kenesaw Mountain, Ga., June 27, 1864. Buried in Marietta National Cemetery; grave marked "Hiram Wilcox."

Andrew Heller, Co. E, 113th O. V. I., died in field hospital, near Atlanta, Ga., Aug. 13, 1864. Buried in Marietta National Cemetery.

Wallace Hogarth, Co. B, 113th O. V. I., wounded at Bentonville, N. C., March 19, 1865; died March 20, 1865. Buried in National Cemetery at Wilmington, N. C., as Unknown.

John W. Hall, Co. H, 45th O. V. I., died at Danville, Ky., March 24, 1863. Buried at home.

John Hudson, Co. D, 134th O. N. G., died at Hampton, Va., Aug. 6, 1864. Buried in Hampton National Cemetery.

E. Harrison Hovey, Co. A, 2d O. V. I., wounded at Perryville, Ky., Oct. 8, 1862; died at Murfreesboro, of pneumonia, Mch. 23, 1863. Buried in Stone River National Cemetery; grave marked "E. H. Harrison."

John Hobson, Co. L, 2d Heavy Artillery, prisoner of war, died at Danville, Va., Jan. 10, 1865. Buried in Danville National Cemetery.

John Henry, Co. B, 32d O. V. I., died at Vicksburg, Miss., June 14, 1864. Buried in Vicksburg National Cemetery.

John Harbour, Co. H, 134th O. N. G., died at Portsmouth, Va., July 6, 1864. Buried at home.

Amos Hoak, Co. C, 13th O. V. I., accidentally killed Jan. 1, 1863, near Murfreesboro, Tenn. Buried in Stone River National Cemetery.

John W. Henry, Co. H, 26th O. V. I., died in Virginia, Oct. 17, 1861. Burial place unknown.

Geo. Huffman, Co. H, 26th O. V. I., died in Virginia, Dec. 13, 1861. Burial place unknown.

Christian Heintz, Co. G, 95th O. V. I., died at Collierville, Tenn., Dec. 20, 1863. Burial place unknown.

Ellery Channing Horr, Co. B, 32d O. V. I., died at Beverly, Va., Dec. 28, 1861. Buried at home.

Levi Hemminger, Co. K, 113th O. V. I.,
wounded at Kenesaw Mountain, Ga.,
June 27, 1864, and died Aug. 1, 1864, at
Chattanooga, Tenn. Buried in Chattanooga National Cemetery; grave marked "Levi Herrington."

James Harman, Co. D. 66th O. V. I., died at
Alexandria, Va., Aug. 10, 1862. Buried
in Alexandria National Cemetery.

Clinton D. Henderson, Co. E, 45th O. V. I.,
was mortally wounded at Knoxville,
Tenn., Nov. 18, 1863, and died Nov. 20,
1863. Buried in Knoxville National
Cemetery as Unknown.

I

John R. Irwin, Co. G, 66th O. V. I., killed at
Cedar Mountain, Va., Aug. 9, 1862. Bu-
ried as Unknown in Culpeper National
Cemetery.

Antrim Idle, Co, C, 13th O. V. I., died Dec.
3, 1862, of injuries received on Railroad.
Buried at home.

Isaiah Idle, Co. B, 61st O. V. I., killed at
Chancellorsville, Va., May 2, 1863. Buried in National Cemetery at Fredericksburg as Unknown.

J

Samuel A. Jones, Co. E, 95th O. V. I., died
at Memphis, Tenn., March 15, 1863.
Buried in Memphis National Cemetery.

Lemuel P. Jones, Co. K., 113th O. V. I,, killed
at Kenesaw Mountain June 27, 1864.
Buried in Marietta National Cemetery.

Eli Johnson, Co. E, 95th O. V. I., died at
home October 17, 1862.

Wm. Jordan, Co. H, 45th O. V. I., captured at Knoxville, Tenn., Nov. 18th, 1863, and died in Andersonville, Ga., prison Aug. 15, 1864.

Truman Jackson, Co. G, 95th O. V. I., lost by the burning of the Sultana, April 27, 1865.

John Julien, Co. K, 99th O. V. I., died at Chattanooga, Tenn., Nov. 10, 1864. Buried in the National Cemetery at that place.

John A. Jones, 13th Ohio Battery, died at Columbus, O., Aug. 29, 1863. Buried in Green Lawn Cemetery.

Stephen F. Johnson. Co. I, 66th O. V. I., was killed Dec. 19, 1864. Place of death unknown.

Thomas J. Johnson, Co. H, 45th O. V. I., killed at Knoxville, Tenn., Nov. 18, 1863. Buried at home.

Geo. A. Johnson, Co. H, 45th O. V. I., died in Atlanta, Ga., Sept. 15, 1864. Buried in Marietta National Cemetery.

C. W. Jackson, Co. H, 134th O. N. G., died on Long Island, N. Y., Aug. 2, 1864. Buried in Cypress Hill National Cemetery.

J. Johnson. Co. D, 134th O. N. G., died at City Point, Va., ——— 1864. Buried in City Point National Cemetery.

Milton Jones, Co. I, 96th O. V. I., died at Milliken's Bend, La., May 30, 1863. Burial place unknown.

Wm. Johnson, Co. G, 66th O. V. I., died on Long Island, N. Y., April 3, 1865. Buried in Cypress Hill National Cemetery.

Samuel Jamison, Co. B, 66th O. V. I., captured by the enemy at Port Republic, Va., June 9, 1862; exchanged Sept. 6, 1862, and died in Washington, D, C., Oct. 6, 1862, from the effects of imprisonment on Belle Isle, near Richmond, Va.

Charles Journell, of Johnson township, died in 1862. Regiment unknown.

K

Isaiah Kline, Co. A, 2d O. V. I., killed at Resacca, Ga., May 14, 1864. Buried in Chattanooga National Cemetery.

Samuel J. B. Kennedy, Co. H, 45th O. V. I., captured by the enemy at Knoxville, Tenn., Nov. 18, 1863, and died in Andersonville prison, Aug. 29, 1864.

James Kelly, Co. H, 2d O. V. I., wounded at Resacca, Ga., May 14, 1864, and died May 15. Buried in National Cemetery at Chattanooga.

David B. Kelch, Co. K, 66th O. V. I., died at Harpers Ferry, Va., Dec. 31, 1862. Buried as Unknown in Winchester National Cemetery.

Joseph Kernes, Co. H, 66th O. V. I., died ———— 1863, at home, of disease contracted in the service.

Thomas B. Kizer, Co. C, 13th O. V. I., killed at Stone River, Tenn., Dec. 31, 1862. Buried at home.

Joseph Kennedy, Co. I, 66th O. V. I., died at Strasburg, Va., May 14, 1862. Buried as Unknown in Winchester National Cemetery.

Robert Kelch, Co. I, 66th O. V. I., wounded
at Chancellorsville, Va., May 3, 1863, and
died in Washington, D. C., May 17, 1863.
Buried in Military Asylum National
Cemetery.

Lewis Keightlinger, Co. I, 66th O. V. I.,
killed at Port Republic, Va., June 9,
1862. Buried in National Cemetery at
Staunton, Va., among the unknown.

John J. Kohler, Co, I, 66th O. V. I., wounded at Antietam, Md., Sept. 19, 1862, and
died Oct. 14, 1862, in field hospital. Buried in National Cemetery on the battle
ground.

Joseph Kitchen, Co. I, 42d O. V. I., died at
Cairo, Ills., about Jan. 11, 1863. Buried
in National Cemetery at Cairo.

Owen B. Kenaga, 13th Ohio Battery, died at
home, May 7, 1862. Buried in Oak Dale
Cemetery.

Moses Kline, Co. A, 2d O. V. I., captured by
the enemy at Chickamauga, Ga., Sept.
20, 1863; died in Andersonville prison,
Sept. 4, 1864. Buried in Andersonville
National Cemetery.

Thomas J. Kirkwood, Co. G, 66th O. V. I.,
died at home, Feb. 11, 1863.

Charles Kelley, Co. C, 13th O. V. I., died at
Urbana,—date unknown.

L

Jos. G. Lloyd, Sergt,, Co. D, 13th O. V. I.,
wounded in charge on Mission Ridge,
Tenn., Nov. 25, 1863; died at Chattanooga, Tenn., Nov. 29, 1863. Buried in
National Cemetery at Chattanooga.

John M. Lane, Co. B, 32d O. V. I., died near Atlanta, Ga., Oct. 19, 1864. Buried in Marietta National Cemetery.

Eli Lemen, Co. I, 42d O. V. I., mortally wounded at Thompson's Hill, Miss., and died May 1, 1863, at Port Gibson. Buried in Vicksburg National Cemetery.

W. P. Long, Co. A, 2d O. V, I., killed at Stone River, Tenn., Dec. 31, 1862. Buried in National Cemetery on the battle ground.

Daniel Leonard, Co. G, 95th O. V. I., died at Bear Creek hospital, Miss., Sept. 16, 1863. Burial place unknown.

James Lodrick, Co. E, 95th O. V. I., wounded June 19, 1863, and died July 5, 1863, on board hospital steamer "Crescent City," Burial place unknown.

Jas. W. Lyon, Co. I, 42d O. V. I., wounded at Chickasaw Bayou, Dec. 29, 1862, and died Jan. 5, 1863. Buried in Vicksburg National Cemetery as Unknown.

John Leuty, Co. H, 45th O. V. I., died in Urbana, Dec. 11, 1864. Buried in Oak Dale Cemetery.

John Ludrick, of Union township, died from disease contracted in the service. Date of death and regiment unknown.

Robert Layton, Co. G, 66th O. V. I., killed at Cedar Mountain, Va., Aug. 9, 1862. Buried in Culpeper National Cemetery among the unknown.

Samuel Legge, Co. I, 66th O. V. I., died after discharge, of disease contracted in the service. Date of death unknown.

J. C. Lessinger, Co. H, 45th O. V. I., died in Kentucky, May 27, 1864. Buried in Camp Nelson National Cemetery, or in Linden Grove Cemetery, Covington, Ky.

John Lapham, Co. C, 2d O. V. I.,—date and place of death unknown.

John B. Lung, Co. H, 45th O. V. I., prisoner of war from Knoxville, Tenn., died at Andersonville, Ga., Aug. 4, 1864.

John M. Loughlin, Co. H, 45th O. V. I., died at Lexington, Ky., April 13, 1864. Buried in Lexington National Cemetery.

George Lyons, Co. H, 134th O. N. G., died at Hampton, Va., Aug. 2, 1864. Buried in Hampton National Cemetery.

H. W. Long, Co. A, 2d O. V. I., killed at Perryville, Ky,, Oct. 8, 1862. Buried at home.

O. D. Lawler, Co. B, 32d O. V. I., died at Marietta, Ga., Sept. 25, 1864. Buried in Marietta National Cemetery.

M

Peter Miller, Co. E, 95th O. V. I., lost in the burning of the steamer Sultana, April 27, 1865. Had been a prisoner at Andersonville.

John McCumber, Co. E, 95th O. V. I., prisoner of war at Andersonville, and died at home, after exchange, April 2, 1865.

Wm. Mott, Co. E, 113th O. V. I., prisoner of war from Chickamauga, confined at Andersonville, Ga., 18 months. Died after discharge, of disease contracted during imprisonment.

Allen McDonald, Co. G, 95th O. V. I., killed at Guntown, Miss., June 10, 1864. Burial place unknown.

Burton Mitchell, Co. G, 95th O. V. I., died at Nashville, Tenn., Feb. 18, 1865. Buried in Nashville National Cemetery.

John O. Minturn, Co. C, 13th O. V. I., drowned in Ohio River, February —, 1862, while returning to his Regiment.

John McAlexander, 20th O. V. I., killed near Atlanta, Ga., July 1, 1864. Buried in Marietta National Cemetery.

Jas. K. McDonald, ——— Ind. Vols., killed in Virginia, July —, 1861. Burial place unknown.

T. J. McArthur, Corp., Co. H, 26th O. V. I., died of small-pox, June 4, 1864. Place of death and burial unknown.

James Miller, Co. H, 26th O. V. I., was wounded at Kenesaw Mountain, Ga., June 27, 1864, and died Aug. 31, 1864. Burial place unknown.

David McCully, Co. A, 66th O. V. I., died at Columbus, O., March 11, 1865. Burial place unknown.

Henry McGale, Co. C, 66th O. V. I., was wounded at New Hope Church, May 25, 1864, and died June 9, 1864, at Chattanooga. Buried in National Cemetery at that place; grave marked "Henry McGall."

Casper Mouser, Co. G, 66th O. V. I., wounded at Antietam, Md., Sept. 17, 1862, and died in field hospital Oct. 10, 1862. Buried in National Cemetery on the battle ground.

Wm. Edward Morris, Co. I, 66th O. V. I., killed at Antietam, Md., Sept. 17, 1862. Buried in National Cemetery on the battle ground.

Irwin Mouser, Co. G, 66th O. V. I., died at Cumberland, Md., Feb. 25, 1862. Buried in Antietam National Cemetery; grave marked "Erwin Nours, Co. B, 66th."

Jno. S. Mitchell, Co. B, 66th O. V. I., died a Fayetteville, N. C., Mch. 13, 1865, on Sherman's march from Savannah to Goldsboro. Buried in National Cemetery at Wilmington, N. C.

Robert Murdoch, Lieut. and Adjutant, 66th O. V. I., shot himself in delirium of fever, at Alexandria, Va., Aug. 25, 1862. Buried in Oak Dale Cemetery.

Jas. H. McBeth, Co. G, 66th O. V. I., died at Alexandria, Va., ——— ———. Buried in National Cemetery at that place.

Patrick Madigan, Co. B, 61st O. V. I., died at Covington, Ky., Jan. 17, 1864. Buried in National Cemetery at that place.

Richard R. McNemar, Co. H, 86th O. V. I., died in Springfield, O., May 27, 1863. Buried in Oak Dale Cemetery.

Elhanan M. Mast, Lieut. Col., 13th O. V. I., killed at Chickamauga, Ga., Sept. 19, 1863. Buried in Chattanooga National Cemetery.

Richard McCarthy, Co. C, 13th O. V. I., died at Gauley, W. Va., Oct. 27, 1861. Burial place unknown.

D. D. Moore, Co. A, 2d O. V. I., prisoner of war from Chickamauga, died at Andersonville, Ga,, Sept. 9, 1864.

Henry Martin, Co. H, 26th O. V. I., wounded at Chickamauga, Ga., Sept. 19, 1863, and died at Chattanooga, Tenn., Oct. 12, 1863. Buried in Chattanooga National Cemetery.

Thomas Moore, Co. C, 13th O. V. I., wounded at Stone River, Tenn., Dec. 31, 1862; died at home, April 8, 1864, of injuries received on cars.

Jas. R. McClure, Co. K, 134th O. N. G., died at Hampton, Va., Aug. 20, 1864 Buried in Hampton National Cemetery.

Peter Miller, Co. E, 113th O. V. I., killed at Stone River, Tenn., Dec. 31, 1862. Buried as Unknown in National Cemetery on the battle ground.

Wm. McManus, Co. I, 113th O. V. I., killed at Tunnel Hill, Ga., May 3, 1864. Buried in Chattanooga National Cemetery.

Elijah Morris, Co. G, 95th O. V. I., died at Memphis, Tenn., June 20, 1865. Buried in Memphis National Cemetery.

Wm. McCoy, (regiment unknown) died at Vicksburg, Miss., June 10, 1863. Buried in National Cemetery at that place.

Alex. McGahan, Co. G, 95th O. V. I., died at Fort Pickering, near Memphis, Tenn., Feb. 21, 1863. Buried in Memphis National Cemetery.

Richard J. McVey, Co. E, 95th O. V. I., died at home, April 23, 1865.

Duncan A. McDonald, 2d Lieut., 66th O. V. I., mortally wounded at Cedar Mountain, Va., Aug. 9, 1862, and died in Alexandria, Va., Aug. —, 1862. Buried in Oak Dale Cemetery.

John W. Martz, Sergt., Co. E, 95th O. V. I.,
died at Bear Creek Hospital, Miss., Sept.
1, 1863. Buried in Vicksburg National
Cemetery

Patrick Murphy, Co. B, 66th O. V. I., killed
at Pine Mountain, Ga., June 15, 1864.
Buried in Marietta National Cemetery.

James McAlexander, Co. H, 134th O. N. G.,
died near Washington, D. C., Aug. 24,
1864. Buried in Arlington National
Cemetery.

Lorenzo D. McElhaney, Co. E, 185th O. V.
I., died at Louisville, Ky., April 28, 1865.
Buried in Cave Hill Cemetery.

Thomas K. Mouser, Co. H, 26th O. V. I.,
wounded and captured at Chickamauga,
Ga., Sept. 19, 1863, and died in prison at
Weldon, N. C., Oct. 13, 1863.

Wm. H. Miller, Co. H, 26th O. V. I., died
March 16, 1865. Place of death and burial unknown.

Wm. McClintock, Co. H, 26th O. V. I., died
near Lavergne, Tenn., ——— ———.
Buried in Nashville National Cemetery.

Ben. K. Miller, Lieut., 45th O. V. I., killed
at Kenesaw Mountain, Ga., June 27,
1864. Buried in Oak Dale Cemetery.

Jeremiah Mahoney, Co. C, 66th O. V. I.,
prisoner of war, died in Richmond, Va.,
July —, 1862. Buried in Richmond National Cemetery.

John McCune, Co. D, 2d O. V. I., was
drowned at Cincinnati, O., Oct. —, 1864,
as the regiment was going to Columbus,
O., for muster-out.

Joseph Meade, Co. D, 2d O. V. I., killed at Perryville, Ky., Oct. 8, 1862. Buried in Perryville National Cemetery.

Thomas McDermott, Corporal, Co. F, 54th O. V. I., was killed at Walnut Hills, Miss., May 19, 1863. Buried in Vicksburg National Cemetery as Unknown.

Wm. A. Miller, Co. F, 54th O. V. I., wounded at Shiloh, Tenn., and died May 10, 1862. Buried in Shiloh National Cemetery.

John Maloney, Co. E, 95th O. V. I., died at West Jefferson, O., June 19, 1863.

Owen Moffitt, Co. A, 66th O. V. I., died at Philadelphia, Pa., Dec. 5, 1862. Buried in National Cemetery at that place.

Uriah S. McRoberts, Co. E, 113th O. V. I., died at home, Oct. —, 1862. Buried in Oak Dale Cemetery.

Perry G. McCandless, 1st Heavy Artillery, died at Camp Nelson, Ky., Jan. 20, 1864. Buried in Camp Nelson National Cemetery.

Azro Mann, Co. K, 113th O. V. I., died at Nashville, Tenn., Oct. 31, 1864. Buried in Nashville National Cemetery.

J. McDowell, Co. E, 113th O. V. I., prisoner of war, died in Danville, Va., April 16, 1864. Buried in Danville National Cemetery.

James McGill, Co. A, 66th O. V. I., died at Washington, D. C., June 24, 1862. Buried in Oak Dale Cemetery.

Malcolm McCallister, —— 110th O. V. I., —date and circumstances of death unknown.

Hector Morren, Co. K, 113th O. V. I., wounded at Kenesaw Mountain, Ga., June 27, 1864; died at Big Shanty, Ga., June 30, 1864. Buried in Marietta National Cemetery.

James McMahan, Co. K, 113th O. V. I., died at Jeffersonville, Ind,, Dec. 23, 1864. Buried in National Cemetery at New Albany.

George Milledge, Corporal, Co., I, 66th O. V. V. I., killed at New Hope Church, Ga., May 27. 1864. Buried in Marietta National Cemetery as Unknown.

Cornell McGill, Co. A, 66th O. V. I., died in Washington, D. C., Oct. —, 1862. Buried in Oak Dale Cemetery.

Zachariah Meeks, Co. H, 66th O. V. I., died at Harpers Ferry, Va., Nov. 10, 1862. Buried as Unknown in Winchester National Cemetery.

John B. McGown, Sergt., Co. G, 66th O. V. I., killed at Port Republic, Va., June 9, 1862. Buried as Unknown in Staunton National Cemetery.

John McClary, Co. D, 66th O. V. I., killed at Gettysburg, Pa., July 3, 1863. Buried in Gettysburg National Cemetery.

Alex. Michael, Co. K, 113th O. V. I., died at home, of disease contracted in the service; date unknown.

Peter Morris, Co. I, 66th O. V. I., discharged ——— ——— and died at home, from disease contracted in the service, ——— 1865.

N

Joseph H. Newcomb, Co. K, 113th O. V. I., died at Nashville, Tenn., July 24, 1864. Buried as Unknown in Nashville National Cemetery.

Wm. Amos Neer, Co. G, 66th O. V. I., killed on the Central Ohio Railroad, near Glencoe, Belmont county, O., Jan. 18, 1862. Buried in Oak Dale Cemetery.

Wm. Nitchman, Sergt., Co. H, 45th O. V. I., prisoner of war from Philadelphia, Tenn., Oct. 20, 1863, died in prison, Richmond, Va., April 18, 1864. Buried in Richmond National Cemetery.

Matthew Newland, Co. H, 26th O. V. I., died Feb. 28, 1862. Place of death and burial unknown.

O

Ephraim Obenour, Co. B, 61st O. V. I., wounded at Gettysburg, Pa., July 1, 1863; died in the hands of the enemy, July 5, 1863. Buried in Gettysburg National Cemetery.

Henry Oman, Co. B, 134th O. N. G., died at City Point, Va., ———, 1864. Buried in City Point National Cemetery.

John R. Organ, Lieutenant, 66th O. V. V. I., wounded at Cedar Mountain, Va., Aug. 9, 1862; killed at Peach Tree Creek, Ga., July 20, 1864. Buried in Marietta National Cemetery.

J. G. Palmer, Major, 66th O. V. I., mortally wounded in front of earthworks on Culp's Hill, near Gettysburg, Pa., July 3, 1863. Died of wounds July 10, 1863. Buried in New York.

Timothy Outram, Co. A, 66th O. V. I., died April 24, 1862. Buried in Winchester National Cemetery.

Robert R. Osborn, Co. K, 113th O. V. I., died at Chattanooga, Tenn., Aug. 22, 1864. Buried in National Cemetery at Chattanooga.

Marion Organ, Co. A, 66th O. V. I., died at home, June 24, 1864.

Patrick O'Brien, Co. E, 95th O. V. I., died at Camp Lew Wallace, near Indianapolis, Ind., Dec. 20, 1862. Burial place unknown.

Ralph Osborn, Co. H, 26t O. V. I., died at Columbus, O., March 28, 1864. Buried in Green Lawn Cemetery at that place.

P

J. G. Palmer, Major, 66th O. V. I., mortally wounded in front of earthworks on Culp's Hill, near Gettysburg, Pa., July 3, 1863. Died of wounds July 10, 1863. Buried in New York.

Wm. H. Powell, Co. B, 66th O. V. I., died at Strasburg, Va., May —, 1862. Buried at home.

S. P. Prettyman, 13th Ohio Battery, died at St. Louis, Mo., May 24, 1862. Buried in Oak-Dale Cemetery.

Geo. F. Pratt, Co. A, 134th O. N. G., died at Washington, D. C., Aug. 3, 1864. Buried at home.

Jarius Purkeypile, Co. E, 95th O. V. I., died Sept. 1, 1863. Place of death unknown.

Wm. Poling, Co. H, 18th O. V. I., died in Chattanooga, Tenn., July 13, 1865. Buried in Chattanooga National Cemetery.

Eli Pence, Co. E, 45th O. V. I., prisoner of war from Philadelphia, Tenn., died in Richmond, Va., March 4, 1864. Buried in Richmond National Cemetery.

J. Patterson, Co. H, 45th O. V. I., prisoner of war, died in Augusta, Ga., July 29, 1864. Buried in Lawton National Cemetery, near Millen, Ga.

James C. Porter, Co. A, 66th O. V. I., killed at Chancellorsville, Va., May 3, 1863. Buried with unknown at Fredericksburg National Cemetery.

Joseph Powell, Co. B, 66th O. V. V. I., killed by a 200-lb. shell from rebel ram "Georgia," in front of Savannah, Ga., Dec. 18, 1864. Buried as Unknown in Lawton National Cemetery, near Millen, Ga.

David S. Price, 13th Ohio Battery, killed at Pittsburg Landing, April 6, 1862, while the battery was taking position. Buried at home.

Jacob Pickerell, Co. E, 95th O. V. I., died at Memphis, Tenn., March 12, 1865. Buried as Unknown in Memphis National Cemetery;—grave marked "Jac. Pickering."

A. Pitman, Co. G, 66th O. V. I., joined for duty Aug. 8, 1862; killed at Cedar Mountain, Va., Aug. 9, 1862. He was dressed in citizen's clothing. Buried with the Unknown in Culpeper National Cemetery.

Wm. A. Powell, Co. B, 66th O. V. I., killed at Cedar Mountain, Va., Aug. 9, 1862. Buried as Unknown in Culpeper National Cemetery.

Henry C. Peterson, Co. E, 95th O. V. I., died at Young's Point, La., May 24, 1863. Burial place unknown.

Geo. Peebles, Co. K, 113th O. V. I., died in Baltimore, Md., April 18, 1865. Buried in Loudon Park Cemetery.

R. B. Parker, Co. E, 113th O. V. I., died at Nashville, Tenn., Feb. 22, 1863. Buried in Nashville National Cemetery.

Wm. H. Protsman, Co. E, 113th O. V. I., died at Nashville, Tenn., March 11, 1863. Buried at home.

Samuel Pullings. Co. D, 66th O. V. I., killed in front of Atlanta, Ga., July 28, 1864. Buried in National Cemetery at Marietta, Ga.

James Peese, Co. D, 2d O. V. I., captured by the enemy at Chickamauga, Ga., Sept. 9, 1863. Date of death unknown.

Clay Pence, Co. K, 12th Ohio Cavalry, killed at Abingdon Salt Works, Va., ——, 1865. Burial place unknown.

John D. Pence, Co. H, 45th O. V. I., died at Covington, Ky., Oct. 8, 1862. Buried in Oak Dale Cemetery.

Samuel W. Poysell, Co. E, 95th O. V. I., lost in burning of steamer Sultana, April 27, 1865.

Wm. W. Poysell, Co. E, 95th O. V. I., lost in burning of steamer Sultana, April 27, 1865.

Jacob Poland, Co. A, 66th O. V. I., wounded at Port Republic, Va., June 9, 1862, and died in Washington, D. C., July 9, 1862. Buried in Military Asylum National Cemetery.

W. E. Parker, Co. H, 45th O. V. I., prisoner of war, died in Andersonville prison, April 25, 1864. Buried in Andersonville National Cemetery.

Wm. M. Patrick, Sergt., Co. G, 3d Ohio Cavalry, killed by guerrillas, while on picket, near Gunthersville, Ala., Aug. 3, 1862. Buried at home.

Joel Pennington, Co. G, 3d Ohio Cavalry, died at Columbia, Tenn., April 11, 1864. Buried in Stone River National Cemetery.

Chas. Proctor, originally of 2d Ohio Inf., joined another regiment and died in the service. Regiment unknown.

James E. Paden, Co. H, 66th O. V. I., died at home, of disease contracted in the service,—date unknown.

John T Petty, 110th O. V. I., killed in Virginia. Place of burial not known.

R

E. B. Rutan, Co. E, 44th O. V. I., died at Andersonvile, Ga., Sept. 2, 1864. Buried in Andersonville National Cemetery.

Abner Read, Commander U. S. Navy, commanding U. S. gunboat Monongahela, wounded at Donaldsville, La., July 7, 1863, and died from the effects of his wounds. He had been in the service 24 years.

Wm. A. Rhoads, Lieut., 36th O. V. I., was wounded at Chickamauga, Ga., Sept. 19, 1863, and died in Chattanooga, Tenn, Oct. 11, 1863. Buried at home.

Amos Richardson, Lieut., 27th U. S. C. T., was killed in charge on a Fort in front of Petersburg, Va., July 30, 1864. No Burial.

J. E. W. Rettberg, 1st Ohio Artillery, killed at Stone River, Dec. 31, 1862. Buried in Oak Dale Cemetery.

A. Ross, Co. H, 45th O. V. I., died in Andersonville prison, March 19, 1864. Buried in Andersonville National Cemetery.

Wm. Read, Co. F, 134th O. N. G., died at Hampton, Va., Aug. 18, 1864. Buried in National Cemetery at Hampton.

Alex. Rhoads, Co. H, 134th O. N. G., died at Hampton, Va., Aug. 16, 1864. Buried in Hampton National Cemetery.

Joseph M. Russell, Corporal, Co. C, 134th O. N. G., died at Hampton, Va., Aug. 10, 1864. Buried at home.

J. T. Ray, Co. B, 134th O. N. G., died at City Point, Va., Aug. 7, 1864. Buried in City Point National Cemetery.

Geo. W. Redman, Co. E, 185th O. V. I., died in Louisville, Ky., March 9, 1865. Buried in Cave Hill National Cemetery.

Marion Ross, Sergeant-Major, 2d O. V. I., was captured by the enemy during a raid in the direction of Atlanta, Ga., in 1862, and was hanged near that city. He is buried in Chattanooga National Cemetery.

Franklin Russell, Co. E, 113th O. V. I., killed at Chickamauga, Ga., Sept. 19, 1863. Buried in Chattanooga National Cemetery.

Jeremiah Richwein, Co. E, 95th O. V. I., died July 27, 1863, on board hospital steamer "Nebraska," of wounds received at Vicksburg July 2, 1863.

Geo. W. Runyon, Co. G, 95th O. V. I., died Oct. 26, 1863, at Vicksburg, Miss. Buried in National Cemetery at that place.

Leonard Roberts, Co. H, 26th O. V. I., died at Camp Ewing, Va., Oct. 28, 1861. Burial place unknown.

Samuel Richeson, Co. H, 26th O. V. I., died at Nashville, Tenn., July 17, 1864. Buried in Nashville National Cemetery.

Wm. Rhoads, Capt., 45th O. V. I., died at home, on recruiting service, Nov. 1, 1863. Buried in Oak Dale Cemetery.

Simon Ryan, Color Corporal, Co. C, 66th O. V. I., was wounded in night charge on the enemy's works, near Pine Mountain, Ga., June 15, 1864. Died at Chattanooga July 21, 1864. Buried in Chattanooga National Cemetery.

Caleb Reams, Co. H, 66th O. V. I., was accidentally killed by a comrade, at Forrer's Furnace, Va., June 10, 1862. Buried as Unknown in Staunton National Cemetery.

Hugh Renold, Co. H, 66th O. V. I., was wounded at Pine Mountain, Ga., June 15, 1864, and died at Chattanooga, Tenn., June 24, 1864. Buried in Chattanooga National Cemetery.

John B. Runyon, Co. A, 66th O. V. I., was
killed at Chancellorsville, Va., May 3,
1863. Buried as Unknown in Fredericksburg National Cemetery.

St. Leger James Rock, Co. D, 66th O. V. I.,
killed at Port Republic, Va., June 9,
1862. Buried in National Cemetery at
Staunton, Va., among the unknown.

Levi Romine, Co. K, 113th O. V. I., killed at
Kenesaw Mountain, Ga., June 27, 1864.
Buried in Marietta National Cemetery.

John Rockey, Co. F, 17th O. V. I., wounded
at Pine Mountain, Ga., June 15, 1864,
and died June 19. Buried in Marietta
National Cemetery.

Jacob Reinsmith, Co. G, 95th O. V. I., died
at Milliken's Bend, La., June 26, 1863.
Burial place unknown.

George H. Rollins, Co. E, 95th O. V. I., was
lost in the burning of the steamer
Sultana, April 27, 1865.

Henry Rea, Corporal, Co. E, 45th O. V. I.,
was killed near Atlanta, Ga., August 23,
1864. Buried in Marietta National Cemetery.

Christopher Ryan, Jr., —— Ky. Cav., died
at home, Jan. 27, 1862. Buried in Oak
Dale Cemetery.

Jac. S. Read, Sergt., Co. C, 12th Ohio Cavalry, died at Chattanooga, Tenn., Aug.
11, 1865. Buried in National Cemetery
at that place.

James C. Reynolds, Co. G, 95th O. V. I., died
of wounds at Richmond Ky. Burial
place unknown.

Jos. K. Ramsey, Co. H, 45th O. V. I., died in prison at Richmond, Va., Feb. 21, 1864. Buried as "J. K. Bormsey," in Richmond National Cemetery.

John Ryan, enlisted in the Regular Army from Union township; died in 1863, in Newport Barracks, Ky.

Calvin Rector, Co. E, 55th Massachusetts Inf., (colored) died in St. Anthony's Parish, S. C. Date and place of burial unknown.

S

Fred. Singer, Color Sergt., Co. H, 26th O. V. I., killed at Stone River, Dec. 31, 1862. Buried in National Cemetery on the battle ground.

Wm. Stone, Co. I, 134th O. N. G., died at Hampton, Va., Aug. 14, 1864. Buried in Hampton National Cemetery.

C. M. Smith, Co. F, 134th O. N. G., died at Portsmouth, Va., July 28, 1864. Buried in Hampton National Cemetery.

Samuel Shoemaker, Co. E, 185th O. V. I., died in Louisville, Ky., April 22, 1865. Buried in Cave Hill National Cemetery.

Anderson Smith, Co. A, 27th U. S. Colored Troops, was killed in charge on Fort in front of Petersburg, Va., July 30, 1864. No burial.

Theo. Sutphon, Co. A, 2d O. V. I., wounded at Stone River, Tenn., Dec. 31, 1862, and died Jan. 12, 1863. Buried in Stone River National Cemetery.

Robert J. Stewart, Lieut., 12th Ohio Cavalry, died in Tennessee, July 31, 1864. Burial place unknown.

Jas. L. Shell, Co. H, 2d O. V. I., wounded at Stone River, Tenn., Dec. 31, 1862, and died Jan. 12, 1863. Buried in Stone River National Cemetery.

Daniel Smith, Co. E, 95th O. V. I., killed at Richmond, Ky. Burial place unknown.

Moses Stein, of Jackson township, died in 1862. Regiment unknown.

James Shaffer, of Madriver township, died in 1862. Regiment unknown.

Dennis Shea, Co. C, 12th Ohio Cavalry, was left sick at Salem, N. C., in May, 1865, and is supposed to have died there.

H. H. Shinnamon, Co. E, 26th O. V. I., died at Mound City, Ills., June 28, 1865. Buried in National Cemetery at that place.

Henry C. Scaggs, Co. C, 66th O. V. I., died at Camp Candy, Md., Feb. 4, 1862. Buried at camp, two miles east of New Creek, Va.

Clinton M. Sharp, Co. E, 45th O. V. I., died at Somerset, Ky., April 18, 1862. Buried as Unknown in Mill Springs National Cemetery.

Isaac Swivley, Co. H, 45th O. V. I., died at Camp Nelson, Ky., July 12, 1864. Buried in Camp Nelson National Cemetery.

David Shinnamon, Co. H, 66th O. V. I., died at Cumberland, Md., in 1862. Place of burial unknown.

Alex. Swisher, Co. E, 95th O. V. I., killed at Richmond, Ky., Aug. 3, 1862. Buried as Unknown in National Cemetery at Richmond.

George A. Sargent, Co. E, 95th O. V. I., died at Chickasaw Spring, Miss., June 27, 1865. Buried as Unknown in Shiloh National Cemetery, Pittsburg Landing, Tenn.

Geo. W. Smith, Co. H, 66th O. V. I., died at Camp Candy, Md., Feb. 2, 1862. Buried at home.

James Smith, Co. H, 18th U. S. Inf., died at Chattanooga, Tenn., July 30, 1865. Buried in Chattanooga National Cemetery.

John Slagle, Co. G, 95th O. V. I., a prisoner of war, died in Millen prison. Buried in Lawton National Cemetery, near Millen, Ga., or at Beaufort, S. C.

Peter Stricklin, Co. G, 95th O. V. I., died at Memphis, Tenn., ———, 1863. Buried in National Cemetery at that place.

C. W. Sears, Chaplain, 95th O. V. I., died at home, Aug. 29, 1863. Buried in Spring Grove Cemetery, Cincinnati.

Gibson Stewart, Co. B, 32d O. V. I., died at Huttonville, Va., Oct. 18, 1861. Burial place unknown.

Ira A. Sargeant, Co. E, 95th O. V. I., killed at Vicksburg, Miss., June 19, 1863. Burial place unknown.

Wm. M. Sayer, Co. K, 66th O. V. I., was mortally wounded at Pine Mountain, Ga., June 15, 1864, and died June 17, 1864. Buried in Marietta National Cemetery.

W. R. Smith, Co. G, 95th O. V. I., died June 26, 1863, in Madison Parish, La. Buried in Vicksburg National Cemetery.

Jos. Sutton, Co. C, 66th O. V. I., was killed at Pine Mountain, Ga., June 15, 1864. Buried in National Cemetery at Marietta.

Joseph H. Shepherd, Co. B, 32d O. V. V. I., died at Clifton, Tenn., May 6, 1864. Buried in Shiloh National Cemetery, at Pittsburg Landing, Tenn., as Unknown.

Daniel D. Smith, Co. H, 26th O. V. I., died at Kingston, O., May 1, 1863. Buried at home.

Clifton Sowell, Co. D, 66th O. V. I., killed at Port Republic, Va., June 9, 1862. Buried as Unknown in Staunton National Cemetery.

John Shepherd, Co. G, 3d Ohio Cavalry, died at Corinth, Miss., in 1862. Burial place unknown.

John J. Swisher, Co. B, 66th O. V. I., prisoner of war, died at Lynchburg, Va., (date unknown) and is buried in Poplar Grove National Cemetery, at Petersburg, Va.

Adolphus Stump, Co. H, 26th O. V. I., killed at Chickamauga, Ga., Sept. 19, 1863. Burial place unknown.

John Schmidt, Co. E, 95th O. V. I., killed at Richmond, Ky., Aug. 3, 1862. Buried as Unknown in Richmond (Ky.) National Cemetery.

Henry Summerling, Co. H, 2d O. V. I., died at Grayville, Ga., April 1, 1864. Buried in Chattanooga National Cemetery; grave marked "Henry Summerland."

C. C. Slaven, Co. G, 3d Ohio Cavalry, killed Aug. 10, 1864, near Jonesboro', Ga.

Richard Sullivan, Co. E, 113th O. V. I., died in Savannah, Ga., Jan. —, 1865. Buried in National Cemetery at Beaufort, S. C.

Geo. W. Shlonaker, Co. E, 113th O. V. I., died at Nashville, Tenn., Mch. 20, 1863. Buried in National Cemetery at that place.

Henry C. Scott, Sergt., Co. E, 113th O. V. I., was killed at Kenesaw Mountain, Ga., June 27, 1864. Buried in National Cemetery at Marietta.

Anthony Schimmell, Co. E, 113th O. V. I.. was wounded at the battle of Utoi Creek, Ga., and died Aug. 7, 1864. Buried in Marietta National Cemetery.

John Steiger, Co. D, 13th O. V. I., was killed at Pine Mountain, Ga., June 18, 1864. Buried in National Cemetery at Marietta.

H. M. Snodgrass, Co. I, 66th O. V. I., died in Philadelphia, Pa., Nov. 28, 1862. Buried in Woodlawn, and subsequently removed to Cemetery at Mechanicsburg.

Cornelius Spillman, Co. B, 61st Ohio Inf., killed at Peach Tree Creek, Ga., July 20, 1864. Buried as Unknown in Marietta National Cemetery.

John Scott, Co. G, 3d Ohio Cav., died at Chattanooga, Tenn., June 3, 1863. Buried in Chattanooga National Cemetery.

John Scott, Co. G, 134th O. N. G., died at home, Sept. 7, 1864, of disease contracted in service.

Geo. Standish, Co. D, 134th O. N. G., died at Clarysville, Md., June 29, 1864. Buried at home.

Joseph Swisher, Co. C, 13th O. V. I., was wounded at Carnifex Ferry, Va., in 1861; amputation of leg resulted in his death. Buried at home. He was the first soldier from Champaign county who lost his life in battle.

David T. Swords, Co. C., 13th O. V. I., died Nov. 13, 1861, in Salem township. Buried in Oak Dale Cemetery.

John H. Stokes, Co. H, 66th O. V. I., was wounded at Port Republic, Va., June 9, 1862; amputation of right leg resulted in his death, July 6, 1862. Buried in Military Asylum National Cemetery, at Washington, D. C.

Zane Stevenson, Co C, 13th O. V. I., killed at Jonesboro, Ga., Sept. 1, 1864. Burial place unknown.

Wm. Sutley, Co. H, 45th O. V. I,, prisoner of war, died in Richmond, Va., April 4, 1864. Buried in Richmond National Cemetery.

Alex. Sutley, Co. H, 45th O. V. I., died at Big Shanty, Ga., July 9, 1864. Buried in Marietta National Cemetery.

Stephen Stowe, Co. ——, 45th O. V. I., died in the service—particulars unknown.

Lewis Sheward, Co. E, 95th O. V. I., prisoner of war from Richmond, Ky.. Aug. 30, 1862 ; died in Indiana, May 9, 1863. Buried in Marion Cemetery as Unknown.

David Smith, Co. E, 95th O. V. I., wounded at Richmond, Ky.; prisoner of war at Andersonville, Ga., and died on board Steamship Baltic, April 18, 1865, the day after exchange.

T

Samuel Thompson, ———, 66th O. V. I., buried in National Cemetery at Wilmington, N. C. Date of death unknown.

James Thomas, ———, 17th O. V. I., died after discharge, of disease contracted in service. Date of death unknown.

Wm. Trimble, Co. H, 66th O. V. I., killed at Port Republic, Va., June 9, 1862. Buried among the unknown in Staunton National Cemetery.

Wm. J. Thomas, Co. H, 66th O. V. I., killed at Port Republic, Va., June 9, 1862. Buried in Staunton National Cemetery as Unknown.

Daniel D. Taylor, Co. E, 95th O. V. I., mortally wounded at Vicksburg, Miss., June 19, 1863; died June 22, 1863. Buried in Vicksburg National Cemetery.

Henry Teates, Co. E, 95th O. V. I., died in Andersonville, Ga., and buried in National Cemetery at Andersonville. This may have been Peter Teates, of the same company, who is not accounted for in the muster-out rolls at the Adjutant General's office.

Wm. E. Tullis, Co. G, 134th O. N. G., died at Cumberland, Md., July 9, 1864. Burial place unknown.

A. Tivinning, Co. H, 134th O. N. G., died at Hampton, Va., Aug. 15, 1864. Buried in Hampton National Cemetery.

Geo. Tinsel, 20th Ohio Inf., died on board a hospital boat, near Paducah, Ky., Oct. 11, 1862. Burial place unknown.

Alfred Terry, Co. A, 27th U. S. Colored Troops, was killed in charge on Fort in front of Petersburg, Va., July 30, 1864. No burial.

Eli A. Thomas, Sergt.-Major, 2d Virginia Cav., mortally wounded near Winchester, Va., Aug. 24, 1864. Burial place unknown.

Joseph B. Toomires, ———, 6th O. V. I., was killed at the charge on Mission Ridge, Nov. 25, 1863. Buried at home.

David Thompson, Corporal. 20th Ind. Vols., wounded in the battle of the Wilderness, Va., May 9, 1864, and died in Alexandria, Va., June 1, 1864. Buried in Arlington National Cemetery.

John H. Tritt, Co. I, 42d O. V. I., died at Louisville, Ky., April 14, 1863. Buried in Cave Hill National Cemetery.

James E. Taylor, Co. I, 66th O. V. I., killed on the works at New Hope Church, May 27, 1864. Buried at Marietta, Ga., as Unknown.

Wm. Tonera, Co. H, 66th O. V. I., wounded at Pine Mountain, Ga., June 15, 1864, and died June 21, 1864, at Kingston, Ga. Buried in Marietta National Cemetery.

Wm. Thomas, Co. B, 113th O.°V. I., missing at Kenesaw Mountain, June 27, 1864. Supposed to have been killed.

Milton F. Thomas, Co. B, 32d O. V. I., died Sept. 30, 1863. Place of death and burial unknown.

Mason Tucker, Co. E, 95th O. V. I., died at Milliken's Bend, La., July 2, 1863. Burial place unknown.

Frank Townsend, Co. G, 95th O. V. I., prisoner of war, died at Andersonville, Ga.

Milton G. Terrell, Co. G, 95th O. V. I., died at Vicksburg, Miss., July 30, 1863. Buried in Vicksburg National Cemetery as Unknown.

Samuel C. Taylor, Co. G, 95th O. V. I., died at Fort Gaines, Ala., March 27, 1865. Buried in Mobile National Cemetery as Unknown.

Hamilton M. Terrell, Co. G, 95th O. V. I., died at Vicksburg, Miss., Aug. 10, 1865. Buried as Unknown in Vicksburg National Cemetery.

V

Harvey Vineyard, Co. B, 66th O. V. I., a prisoner of war, died at Lynchburg, Va., July —, 1862. Buried in Poplar Grove National Cemetery, near Petersburg, Va.

Harrison Veach, Co. G, 95th O. V. I., died at Fort Pickering, Tenn., Feb. 20, 1863. Burial place unknown.

W

D. Webb, Co. C, 12th Ohio Cavalry, died at Catlettsburg, Ky., September 12, 1863. Buried at•Catlettsburg.

Benjamin L. Worrell, ———, 17th O. V. I., wounded at Mission Ridge, Nov. 26, 1863, and died of wounds Dec. —, 1863. Burial place unknown.

Wm. Wilson, Co. H, 66th O. V. I., killed at Port Republic, Va., June 9, 1862. Buried as Unknown in Staunton National Cemetery.

Cornelius Ward, Co. H, 66th O. V. I., killed at Port Republic, Va., June 9, 1862. Buried among the unknown in Staunton National Cemetery.

Jos. Walker, Co. G, 3d Ohio Cavalry, died at Tuscumbia, Ala., June 30, 1862. Buried in National Cemetery at Corinth.

Charles Willoughby, Co. G, 95th O. V. I., died at Duckport, La., June 20, 1863. Burial place unknown.

John E. Weaver, Co. D, 2d O V. I., died at Huntsville, Ala., Aug. 15, 1862. Buried as Unknown in Chattanooga National Cemetery.

Cyrus Worden, Co. G, 134th C. N. G., died at Hampton, Va., July 31, 1864. Buried in Hampton National Cemetery.

J. H. Wilson, Co. F, 55th Mass. Inf. (colored) died in Washington, D. C., April 20, 1865.

Joseph Warner, Co. E. 113th O. V. I., died at Jeffersonville, Ind., Jan 11, 1865. Buried in National Cemetery at that place.

Geo. Workman, Co. B, 113th O. V. I., killed by an insane soldier, in South Carolina, Feb. 24, 1865. Burial place unknown.

Wm. K. Wilkerson, Co. F, 134th O. N. G., died at Hampton, Va., Aug. 4, 1864. Buried in Hampton National Cemetery.

John C. Woolly, Co. A, 66th O. V. I., died at home, ————, 1863, of disease contracted in the service.

Wm. Wells, Co. C, 13th O. V. I., died at Nashville, Tenn., Mch. 19, 1863. Buried in Nashville National Cemetery.

John Weiderman, Co. A, 66th O. V. I., died
at Strasburg, Va., April 21, 1862. Buried
as Unknown in Winchester National
Cemetery.

Aden H. Wood, Color Sergt., Co. C, 13th O.
V. I., was killed at Stone River, Tenn.,
Dec. 31, 1862. Buried in National Cem-
etery on the battle ground.

Michael W. Walker, Co. C. 13th O. V. I., was
wounded at Cassville, Ga., May 19, 1864,
and died May 20, 1864. Burial place
unknown.

Emerson Williams, Co. K, 134th O. N. G.,
died at Hampton, Va., Aug. 15, 1864.
Buried in Hampton National Cemetery.

Andrew J. Ward, Co. E, 113th O. V. I., died
at Nashville, Tenn., July 18, 1863. Buried in Nashville National Cemetery.

Harrison Walburn, Co. E, 113th O. V. I.,
died at Nashville, Tenn., March 5, 1863.
Buried at home.

Joseph Wilkinson, Co. K, 113th O. V. I., was
killed at Kenesaw Mountain, Ga., June
27, 1864. Buried in Marietta National
Cemetery.

John M. Williams, Co. H, 26th O. V. I., was
mortally wounded at Chickamauga, Ga.,
Sept. 1, 1863, and died Oct. 1, 1863. Buried in Chattanooga National Cemetery
as Unknown.

Thomas Whalen, Color Corporal, Co. C, 66th
O. V. V. I., was mortally wounded at
Pine Mountain, Ga., June 15, 1864, and
died at Nashville, Tenn., July 14, 1864.
Buried in Nashville National Cemetery.

Geo. W. Wallace, Sergt., Co. D, 66th O. V. V. I., died at Chattanooga, Tenn., May 20, 1864. Buried in National Cemetery at that place.

· Wesley Wynkook, Co. I, 66th O. V. I., died at Chattanooga, Tenn., June 24, 1864. Buried in National Cemetery at Chattanooga.

John Wren, Co. A, 66th O. V. I., died at Chattanooga, Tenn., July 7, 1864. Buried in National Cemetery at that place.

Matthew Wilson, Co. H, 66th O. V. I., was killed at Kenesaw Mountain, Ga., June 27, 1864. Buried in Marietta National Cemetery.

John Walker, Co. B, 66th O. V. I., was killed at Antietam, Md., Sept. 17, 1862. Buried as Unknown in National Cemetery on the battle ground.

W. H. H. Weaver, Co. B, 66th O. V. I., died at Winchester, Va., ———, 1862. Buried at home.

Geo. C. Wallace, Co. G, 66th O. V. I., died at Alexandria, Va., July 16, 1862. Buried in Alexandria National Cemetery.

Alfred Whittredge, Sergt., Co. C, 12th Ohio Cavalry, was killed at Mt. Sterling, Ky., June 12, 1864. Burial place unknown.

Caleb M. Winget, Corporal, Co. A, 2d O. V. I., was killed at Stone River, Dec. 31, 1862. Buried in National Cemetery on the battle field.

Wm. West, Co. A, 2d O. V. I., killed at Perryville, Ky., Oct. 8, 1862. Buried in Perryville National Cemetery.

J. Webster, Co. B, 32d O. V. I., wounded at
Harpers Ferry, Va., Sept. 14, 1862, and
died at Camp Parole, near Annapolis,
Md., Oct. 2, 1862. Buried in Camp
Parole National Cemetery.

Cyrus Wharton, Co. G, 134th O. N. G., died
at Fortress Monroe, Va., July 31, 1864.
Buried at home.

Frank Willoughby, Co. G, 95th O V. I., was
killed at Richmond, Ky., Aug. 3, 1862.
Buried as Unknown in National Cemetery at that place.

John Whittey, Co. G, 66th O. V I., was killed at Pine Mountain, Ga., June 15, 1864.
Buried in Marietta National Cemetery
as Unknown.

Y

Wm. A. Yutesler, Co. E, 45th O. V. I., died
in Andersonville prison.

Jason Yutesler, of Johnson township, died
in 1862. Regiment unknown.

Additions and Corrections.

The following additions and corrections are published in order to complete the Record of deaths. The compilation of the list has been a laborious task, but since it makes a most valuable link in the permanent history of the county, we feel requited for the work bestowed upon it. We hope it is complete, for the figures show a fearful contribution of lives from this small county, and the list proves a fact we have always maintained, viz: that in proportion, Champaign gave more of her bone and sinew to the country in the time of peril, than any other county in the State.

ADDITIONS.

Dr. Thomas P. Bond, Surgeon, 66th O. V. I., and subsequently of the 32d O. V. I., died at home, in March, 1866, of disease contracted in the service.

Charles Blue, regiment unknown, died in the service; date and place unknown. Buried in Mechanicsburg Cemetery.

John Caton, Co. F, 1st O. V. I., died at Nashville, Tenn., September —, 1862. Buried as Unknown in Nashville National Cemetery.

Charles M. Chester, Co. D, 1st O. V. I., wounded at Rocky-Face Ridge, Ga., May 8, 1864, died at Chattanooga, Tenn., May 27, 1864. Buried in Chattanooga National Cemetery.

Geo. W. Deavers, Co. B, 21st Ills. Inf., prisoner of war, died in Andersonville prison, Ga., April 4, 1864. Buried in Andersonville National Cemetery.

Taylor Darrow, Co. E, 95th O. V. I., died in the service—date and place unknown.

Nelson Durand, Co. H, 66th O. V. I., died in Columbus, O., September —, 1864. Burial place unknown.

James Duffy, Co. H, 45th O. V. I., prisoner of war at Andersonville, Ga., exchanged and died at Camp Parole, Md., Dec. 19, 1864. Buried in National Cemetery at Annapolis.

Geo. Duffy, Co. H, 45th O. V. I., prisoner of war, died at Andersonville, Ga., Sept. 27, 1864. Buried in Andersonville National Cemetery.

John Elbert Ellsworth, Co. —, 5th Ohio Cavalry, wounded in battle of Five Forks, Va., April 9, 1865, and died a few days thereafter at Petersburg. Buried as Unknown in Poplar Grove National Cemetery.

John B. Graham, Sergt., Co. G, 1st O. V. I., died at Chattanooga, Tenn., Dec. 4, 1863, of wounds received at Chickamauga, Ga. Buried in National Cemetery at that place.

John Garrison, —— U. S. Sharpshooters, killed in battle in Virginia,—date and place unknown.

Lorenzo Krouse, Co. —, 44th O. V. I., died in Pennsylvania, ———, 1864, after discharge, of disease contracted in the service.

Reuben Gardner, Co. E, 113th O. V. I., died at home, March —, 1863, of disease contracted in the service. Buried at home.

Isaac Groves, Co. D, 66th O. V. I., died in the service,—date unknown. Buried in Mechanicsburg Cemetery.

Thomas Hanger, of Harrison township, died in the service in 1865. Date and circumstances unknown.

Wm. Hoffman, Co. E, 10th O. V. I., died of wounds received in battle,—date and place unknown.

Samuel Jonnson, Marine, died on a gunboat on the Ohio river,—date unknown. Buried in Mechanicsburg Cemetery.

Melvin Kenfield, Co. K, 2d O. V. I., (three months) Co. A, 2d O. V. I., (three years) prisoner of war from Stone River, Tenn., died in Andersonville prison,—date unknown.

Hugh Knight, Co. D, 66th O. V. I., died in the service,—date and place unknown.

James Kennedy, of Goshen township, died in the service, in an Illinois Regiment,—date and place unknown.

Richard Lansdale, Co. E, 39th O. V. I., died in the service, — date and place unknown.

Patrick Murray, Co. K, 1st O. V. I., was killed at Resacca, Ga., May 14, 1864. Buried in National Cemetery at Chattanooga, Tenn., as Unknown.

Wm. J. Moore, Marine service on gunboat "Brilliant," died Mch. 3, 1866, of disease contracted in the service. Buried at Kingston.

Harrison Owen, Co. I, 66th O. V. I., died at
Camp Chase. near Columbus, O.,—date
unknown. Buried in Mechanicsburg
Cemetery.

Warrett Owens, Lieutenant, 20th O. V. I.,
died at home, of disease contracted in
the service. Date unknown.

George H. Poorman, Co. H, 2d Bat. 18th U.
S. Infantry, wounded at Chickamauga,
Ga., Sept. 20; died Sept. 21, 1863.
Buried in National Cemetery at Chat-
tanooga, Tenn.

James Stanage, Co. C, 93d Ills. Inf., died at
St. Louis, Mo., Nov. 8, 1863. Buried in
National Cemetery at Jefferson Barracks.

George Smith, Co. I, 66th O. V. I., died in
the service,—place and date unknown.
Buried in the Cemetery at Mechanicsburg.

Fred. Singer, Color Sergt., Co. H, 26th O. V.
I., killed at Stone River, Dec. 31, 1862.
Buried in National Cemetery on the
battle ground.

Wm. Stone, Co. I, 134th O. N. G., died at
Hampton, Va., Aug. 14, 1864. Buried in
Hampton National Cemetery.

C. M. Smith, Co. F, 134th O. N. G., died at
Portsmouth, Va., July 28, 1864. Buried
in Hampton National Cemetery.

Samuel Shoemaker, Co. E, 185th O. V. I.,
died in Louisville, Ky., April 22, 1865.
Buried in Cave Hill National Cemetery.

Anderson Smith, Co. A, 27th U. S. Colored
Troops, was killed in charge on Fort in
front of Petersburg, Va., July 30, 1864.
No burial.

Theo. Sutphon, Co. A, 2d O. V. I., wounded at Stone River, Tenn., Dec. 31, 1862, and died Jan. 12, 1863. Buried in Stone River National Cemetery.

Robert J. Stewart, Lieut., 12th Ohio Cavalry, died in Tennessee, July 31, 1864. Burial place unknown.

Luther Taylor, Co. I, 66th O. V. I., died in the service,—date unknown. Buried in Mechanicsburg Cemetery.

Lemuel M. Neal, Co. A, 66th O. V. I., 86th O. V. I., (three months,) and 134th, O. N. G , died in 1864 of disease contracted in the service.

CORRECTIONS.

Wm. R. Arrowsmith, Co. H, 45th O. V. I. There is a discrepancy in the records, and the best evidence we have is that he died April 27, 1864, instead of September 27, as published in the regular list.

Amos Clark, 13th O. V. I., reported dead, is living in the west.

Benj. Herr, Co. G, 95th O. V. I. is buried at home, the family having removed his remains from the National Cemetery at Vicksburg.

Thomas B. Kizer, Co. C, 13th O. V. I., reported buried at home, is buried in the National Cemetery at Stone River, Tenn.

Charles Kelley, 13th O. V. I., reported dead, is living in Iowa.

E. M. Mast, Lt. Col., 13th O. V. I , is buried in the Cemetery at Kingston.

Wm. McCoy, reported "regiment unknown," probably belonged to the 54th O. V. I., and was killed in a charge on the enemy's works at Vicksburg.

Jos. II. Newcomb, Co. K, 113th O. V. I., is buried in Mechanicsburg Cemetery.

Jno. O. Minturn, recorded as of the 13th O. V. I., was enlisted in the 12th Ohio Infantry.

Wm. H. Miller, Co. H, 26th O. V. I., reported "place of death and burial unknown," died in Columbus, O., and is buried in Green Lawn Cemetery.

George W. Shlonaker, Co. E, 113th, O. V. I , is buried in the grave yard at Myrtle Tree Creek Church, near St. Paris, having been removed from Nashville, Tenn.

Dav. T. Swords, Co. C, 13th O. V. I., is buried at Kingston, instead of Oak Dale.

Daniel Smith, Co. E, 95th O. V. I., buried at Woodstock.

Wm. E. Tullis, reported as belonging to Company G, 134th, was a member of Co. C.

Wm. Wells, reported as belonging to Co. C, 13th O. V. I., was not a member of that Company.

Cyrus Worden, Co. G, 134th O. N. G., reported in Government Roll of Honor, is believed to have been Cyrus Wharton.

LOSS BY COMPANIES AND REGIMENTS.

	Killed in battle.	Died by Wounds.	Died in Confederate Prisons.	Died by Disease.	Died by Accident on Water.	Totals.
2d O. V. I., A	11	4	3	2		20
——	2	2	1	4	2	11
3d Cavalry	5			11		16
12th Cavalry	3	2		5		10
13th Infantry	7	4		6	1	18
26th Infantry	5	4	1	15		25
32d Infantry		2		10		12
42d Infantry	2	2		4		8
45th Infantry	6	1	17	14		38
66th Infantry, A	8	4	2	14		28
B	6	1	3	8		18
C	4	5	4	7		20
D	5			4		9
G	8	5		9		22
H	9	1		16		26
I	8	6		15		29
K		1		4		5
——	4	2		1		7
95th Infantry, E	5	3	6	16	4	34
G	3	5	2	22	1	33
113th Infantry, E	6	2	2	12		22
K	9	3		9		21
——	7	2		1		10
134th O. N. G.	1	1		31		33
Colored Troops	5			3		8
Miscellaneous Organizations	22	16	7	49	1	95

TABLE OF RANK AND FILE.

Officers.. 16
Enlisted....................... 562

TOTAL LOSSES IN THE COUNTY.

Killed in battle...... 151
Died of wounds............... 78
  " in Confederate prison........................... 48
  " by drowning... 3
  " " steamboat explosion 6
  " " disease 292
————
Total deaths from the county......................... 578

ORGANIZATIONS REPRESENTED.

INFANTRY.

Ohio:—1st, 2d, 6th, 10th, 13th, 14th, 17th, 18th, 20th, 24th, 26th, 31st, 32d, 33d, 36th, 39th, 40th, 42d, 44th, 45th, 54th, 61st, 66th, 86th, 95th, 99th, 113th, 134th.

CAVALRY.

3d, 4th, 5th, 12th.

ARTILLERY.

2d Heavy, 13th Battery, 17th Battery.

www.ingramcontent.com/pod-product-compliance
Lightning Source LLC
Chambersburg PA
CBHW021513090426
42739CB00007B/598